The Pheasant
in the Tree

The Wisdom of Fritz

Dr. Vreneli Kuhn Wilson

Wilson Reading and Learning
La Jolla, California

The Pheasant in the Tree: The Wisdom of Fritz

For information: drvreneliwilson@aol.com

Design and layout by Silvercat, Encinitas, California

ISBN-13 978-0-9996653-7-4

CONTENTS

FOREWORD
by Robert Goodman

Stories have power. Written or spoken, stories connect the storyteller's private experience to the public context of the story. A story has the overall flavor of the experience, but it represents the storyteller's unique perceptions of the event. The story is universal because it reflects a reality to which everyone can relate. At the same time, the story is intimate because it reveals personal lessons and places them in a mirror where everyone can appreciate their impact.

Vreneli Wilson has written a book full of meaning that goes far beyond its seemingly narrow scope. This book shared much with memoir, history, and biography, though it is none of those genres. It highlights the moments and events that stand out to this day in Verneli Wilson's memory of growing up on a farm in the California's Imperial Valley in the middle of the last century. From the perspective of today, Vreneli can look over her life and share the times and events that proved to be important moments in her life.

Like a memoir, these collected stories share the personal experiences that the author considers valuable passages in her life. These significant moments weave themselves together into a coherent narrative. Unlike a memoir, however, these stories stand on their own. While they highlight certain themes in Wilson's life, they do so as independent anecdotes and vignettes of her early days. You don't need to read the whole book to see the connections among all the stories.

Like a history, the book finds importance behind even the most ordinary events. The Imperial Valley has long been one of California's important agriculture areas. Vreneli Wilson witnessed the valley's evolution during the 20th century. At the same time, she shares personal stories that could only have taken place under private and idiosyncratic circumstances. Even though the stories describe work on the farm or the building of the central aqueduct, they still belong to Vreneli and her family. They put her personal reminiscences in the context of the universal facts of history.

What makes these stories stand out is that none of them is made up. Each story describes a real event or real epiphany in the life of one person. Each reader will feel a unique relationship with each story, and each reader will relate to these stories in his or her own way. That's part of what makes these stories so vital. Different readers will react in different ways, yet readers will understand that the events are true and the reactions are all believable.

Vreneli Wilson's experiences are hers and hers alone. They are private experiences, but they speak volumes about a time in the past when people's work, play, and interpersonal dealings occurred in a time and place very similar to yet very different from what we might expect today. These stories shed light on the nature of personal experience and the social context in which it played itself out.

INTRODUCTION

His name is Fritz Kuhn, Sr. I called him "Vati," an endearing Swiss name, which, when translated, means "Father." He was my Vati since my birth, Christmas day, December 25, 1931.

It was not so much *what* Vati taught me, but *how* he taught me. Much of it was ingrained, but really did not surface to my mind until I became an adult. As I remembered more and more of the lessons, I recollected others he instilled in me.

Vati was a strong but kind man who was both my mother and my father. Early on I knew my mother only as a person afflicted with Huntington's Disease, a terrible disease that affects the whole body.

When you met my father, you would see the twinkle in his eyes that translated into curiosity, mischief, and intrigue. He always wanted to know more about you. He loved to dance, sing, yodel, and tell stories.

Vati was an avid hunter and fisherman. Because of his love of the outdoors, he also was a master cook. No one could cook game like my father. Deer meat marinated in red wine, pheasant stuffed with hamburger spiced with onions, garlic and of course, red wine, stuffed quail, and dove are some of the delicacies I will never forget.

As he cooked, I still see him with a dish towel over his shoulder and a glass of red wine in his hand. He would look at the wine as he twirled it in the glass, then take a sip but not swallow it. He danced his tongue around the wine and then slowly let it roll down this throat.

Wine was always a part of his cooking. Even vanilla ice cream or red, red strawberries were drizzled with wine or cognac.

I want to share Vati with you in hopes that you too will learn some of the teaching styles that seemed so natural to him. Some stories are strong, some have humor, but in all there is something to learn. The twinkle in his eyes made even the deeper learnings a gift.

Fritzi, Vreneli, and the

Imperial Valley Farms

It was on Christmas day in 1931 in Imperial Valley, that I, Vreneli Erika Kuhn, was born. My brother, Fritz Werner Kuhn, was born exactly two years earlier, in 1929, and also on Christmas Day. The rural McCabe area, just outside of El Centro, was Fritzi and my birthplace. Later we moved to rural Seeley, a little one-horse village just west of El Centro. From Seeley we moved back to a different rural area in McCabe and then back to Seeley. Each of these moves was to farm land where we had our small dairy and farm animals.

We grew alfalfa for our cows. From the alfalfa we also made hay for days when the cattle could not go to pasture. It rarely rained in Imperial Valley, giving our Holstein cows many sunny days to graze in the alfalfa fields. At times we had to feed the cows hay, because the grazing fields were too wet from the fields having just been irrigated. The cows' hooves would have destroyed the delicate alfalfa plants.

On the farm we also raised chickens, a couple of pigs for our own butchering, a goat, a couple of sheep, work horses, saddle horses and new born calves. It is easy to see, that although we were not blessed with much money, we certainly had enough food. Vati, my father, made sure that our garden grew an abundance of varied vegetables. During the depression about all we had to buy were coffee, sugar, salt, and flour. The newspapers continually reminded us of the hardship of families living in the cities. God blessed us well.

The Pheasant in the Tree

I'm out in the yard on a sunny day when I notice my father approaching me from having just finished the last of his morning milking. He seems to have a few spare moments. That's not always a good sign.

"Vreneli, come here," he says. I have no idea what's in store, but something interesting was about to take place. I knew that for sure. After all, seven years of life gave me a world of insight to know when intrigue was in the making. What I was always uncertain of was the outcome.

Look at the big tree down by the South Twenty. Do you see the large branch that flows off to the left?" he asked. "Look at the middle one. Do you see it?" he questioned.

"Yes," I responded, feeling confident that I was in his good graces.

"Now, look very, very closely," he continued. "Do you see the pheasant sitting on that tall branch?" he asked.

I wasn't quite sure which branch he meant. I saw no bird of any kind. Being left-handed, I often have trouble with left and right. When this gave me a problem, I would begin to salute the flag. The right hand automatically went over my heart. I did this. I had my directions correct. The left hand unfalteringly stayed at my left side. I looked at my father for the twinkle in his eyes when he had a little mischief in the making. His expression was dead serious. I looked at the branch a little longer. Still, I saw no pheasant in the tree.

"I don't see where you are pointing," I said rather weakly.

"Look…look…just look," he said again.

I squinted my eyes, wanting desperately to see what he saw. The pheasant just wouldn't appear. I tried to envision him flying off so that my father would say, "Oh, he's gone. He just flew away." Then of course I would no longer have to see him, but this didn't happen.

With more determination my father said, "Now look. Follow my finger to where I am pointing…there on the middle branch, halfway up the tree. His head is facing east and his tail is pointing to the west. Do you see it now?" He asked.

In desperation and with a deep need to please, I dramatically announced "Oh, yes! He's beautiful.

His head is looking to the east and his tail is pointed west," I mimicked. "I see him! I see him!" I continued with the drama.

Immediately, my father took on a new stance. He spread apart his legs, held his arm at his waist, and with his right hand he pointed his finger into my face and said, "Don't you ever, ever, ever let anyone talk you into seeing something that you do not see! Pheasants don't perch in trees. They harbor in low-cut brush, grass, and bushes." And with that he walked away, knowing another valuable lesson had been taught.

THE GOPHER SNAKE

lt was between three-thirty and four o'clock in the morning when I felt a massive hand gingerly shake my shoulder. "Vreneli, Vreneli," I heard my father say.

"Vas? Vas?" I replied in Swiss.

"Get up, and come with me," my father went on. "You must hurry or it will be too late."

Frances, my father's horse, was saddled at the front door to our simple, wooden farm house. Vati lifted me into the saddle, and then, with the grace of a John Wayne, Dad slung his leg over Frances and without any groping, his boot landed in the stirrup. Dad was watering the newly planted alfalfa. It was early spring. He had come across a gopher snake, a reptile that was highly prized in Imperial Valley. Gophers were not animals that were liked by Valley farmers. They dug endless tunnels that peered in the middle of an alfalfa field. In the outer side of their cheeks, these rodents had huge pouches in which they carried away dirt to make their canals. As the farmers irrigated their land, the priceless water went into these tunnels and was diverted to roads and fields where water was not needed or wanted and into vacant land. Farmers saw gophers not only as a nuisance, but also as costly. Gopher snakes were allies to the farmers. They consumed many of the rodents. I remember Vati saying many times, "Don't ever kill a snake, it may be a gopher snake."

But what was going on so early in this morning? I was well aware that when the alfalfa needed irrigating, water was ordered from the zanjero several days in advance. The zanjero opened a main gate from the irrigation system and water flowed into our self-made ditches. These ditches ran at the head of our fields where Vati opened a smaller head gate made of concrete. This let water run freely into each lane of alfalfa, my father controlling and changing the water flow to different lanes. Often it took two days to irrigate a whole field. Water from the main source was never shut off until the whole field was watered. Night irrigation was no different than day. Coal oil lantern, a shovel, and gloves were the tools of the trade.

As Frances trotted down to the South Twenty, Vati clued me in on my "nocturnal schooling."

"Remember how many times I told you that you must never, never kill a gopher snake?' my now professor father asked me.

"Yah, yah," I nodded, still half asleep.

Frances headed toward the burning lantern. Vati left it at the lane where he had last been shoveling. Next to it, piercing into the lush Imperial Valley sand, stood his shovel. Vati dismounted and firmly placed his hands under my armpits and gently lifted me to the ground. I was still wearing my pajamas with the chewed rubber buttons. Dad guided me toward a dirt border that held the water between the lanes. I jumped back in fright when I saw a strange tube that looked more like a Polish sausage.

"That," my father began, "is a gopher snake that has just eaten a gopher and was on his second helping." From its mouth protruded the tail and the back end of a gopher. I can still see the rodent being inched into the belly of the whale. I stared for about fifteen or twenty minutes until the last of the tail disappeared.

"How do you know the snake has eaten two gophers," I questioned.

"Look carefully at the tail end of the snake. Notice how much like a snake it looks.

Now look where his body immediately balloons, then how it is very slender again. Do you see that?" my father asked as he pointed to the parts of the snake's anatomy, stopping at the middle slender part. With his finger, Vati emphasized the now enlarged part again. "This," he said, "is the head of the second gopher. He swallows it whole and it will be digested later. Those two gophers could have done a tremendous amount of damage to the field next to this one. When the dairy cows get up and walk in the wet alfalfa field they would have destroyed much of the delicate new plants now used for grazing," he added. We—Frances, Vati, and I—rode back in silence, the snake enjoying his consumption and I digesting a vision that would stay with me for the rest of my life.

THE RUNAWAYS

Today nothing was going right. I couldn't do what I wanted. I was in everyone's way. Fritzi and I did nothing but fight and argue. It was a good day to run away from home. I mentioned my plan to Fritzi. For once, he was in agreement. He thought it a good idea. There was one problem. He wanted a piece of the action. I thought for a moment and then concluded that I might need a hired hand.

We began to plot. Supplies were a dire need. Fritzi got the Red Ryder wagon. Like ants, we began to haul things from the house...food, blankets, matches. My father looked on at our bucket brigade. "What are you two up to?" He asked.

"Oh, we're running away from home," Fritzi stated with an abundance of self assurance.

"You'll need more than two apples, a blanket, and matches," my father said. "Here, let me get a frying pan, some eggs, a little salt and pepper, and a couple of plates. You'll also need some extra socks and an umbrella in case it rains," he continued.

This was beginning to be better than a picnic, I thought. And before too long we were off to the South Twenty like two nomadic hoboes. The "hired hand" pulled the wagon, and I carried and dragged all things that fell from the Red Ryder. At our heels were Waldi and Sebella. Following the two dogs came Baa-Baa, our panting lamb-turned-sheep, who thought she was a dog.

It wasn't easy trudging through the Imperial Valley sand and along the bank of the canal, that carried water to irrigate our alfalfa fields. We stopped often, remarking that the dogs and Baa-Baa needed to rest. Our own little six- and eight-year-old legs were aching.

When we arrived at the South Twenty, a good quarter of a mile from our sheltered home, we rested again, for the sake of the animals, of course. After we caught our breath, we set up camp under the old salt leaf tree. Setting up camp entailed unloading Red Ryder.

Gathering twigs and branches for the fire that was to cook our meal was the next order of business. We dug a shallow hole and placed the twigs and branches in a crisscross manner, a method we saw Vati do many times during our hunting trips with him. Vati had never differentiated tasks normally assigned to women or men. He, himself, was an excellent cook, especially of game. Not knowing that I was to cook and Fritzi was to be the builder of fires, we both broke eggs into the black iron frying pan. Now to ignite the twigs. We both got out the Diamond Matches from the box, and Fritzi made sure that I observed the warning, "Close box before striking match." What he didn't know was that I couldn't read. At that time I couldn't even speak English. We lit match after match, yet the kindling didn't take. But the eggs were already in the pan. How were we to cook them? Summer sun in Imperial Valley could easily parch eggs if left in the sun. We tried. I guess it just wasn't summer enough. Waldi and Sebella salivated at the now warm, but uncooked eggs. We got out the plates, slid the raw eggs on the platters and placed them at front feet of each dog. Fritzi and I satisfied ourselves with two rosy Macintosh apples that by now were also a wee bit warm. At the edge of our flameless campfire, we saw Baa-Baa munching on alfalfa leaves. Our adventure was complete. God gifts children with a sense of completion. There was no need to save face. Our original mission to run away from home needed no further discussion.

I saw the binoculars on the kitchen table. To this day I still wonder it Vati was looking out the window making sure all was well with his two disgruntled hoboes who were obviously hobnobbing with destiny. I saw the binoculars on the kitchen table.

Eggs as a Lesson

On our farm we grew and raised many farm commodities. Some we used for our own table and when there was more than we needed it was sold. Eggs from our range-free chickens was such an item. Gathering them and finding where the hens had laid them became a daily challenge.

Not only did we have to gather them, but next came the chore of candling them. This meant that with a special apparatus that housed a light bulb, we had to look at each egg to make sure they were not old or had been "gifted" with a baby chick. When this was done we assembled an egg carton in which we then put an insert of openings that were three by four.

We sold our eggs to the local grocery store run by a man from China. At a young age it was hard for me to fathom why Vati had to work so hard, when all he had to do was write out a check and Mr. Chang gave him cash. What a blessing was the naivety of the young.

Often when we made one of our egg sale run, Vati also bought the few things we did not raise on our farm such coffee, sugar and flour. On our way to the store, never wanting to waste a moment and capitalizing on learning, Vatti would drill Fritzi with multiplication problems.

"What is three times four," Vati would ask Fritzi. "Having trouble?" He would ask. "Look at one of the boxes of eggs." He would hint. "Three eggs are on the left side of the box and four at the top. Now tell me." He demanded

"Ah, twelve," my brother answered.

"And what is another name for 'twelve'"? Vati asked.

"One dozen...one dozen eggs." Fritzi responded.

And so it went with each trip as our Chevy took us to the store. Sometimes Vati would quiz Fritzi with, "If eggs are twenty cents a dozen and we have six dozen, how much money must Mr. Chang give us?" Vati wanted to know.

Vati had all kinds of short cuts in math which he discussed with Fritzi. My brother became a math whiz. Teachers were amazed.

As for me, math has not been and still is not my forte. I do well in reasoning, but for a solution I need time. Vati was very patient with me.

Eggs were a pivotal learning key to Fritzi and learning math reasoning. One never knows the true value of eggs.

Not Just Peanuts

Honesty was a strong virtue in my father's life. He practiced and modeled it and demanded it of Fritzi and me. We were taught to always do our best and never to cheat.

One day, as we were on our way to Mr. Chang's grocery store to sell several dozens of eggs in our Chevrolet, my father did his usual number task with Fritzi.

"How much must Mr. Chang give us for the seven dozen eggs, if he offers us fifty cents a dozen?" This went on between Vati and Fritzi until we got to Mr. Chang's grocery store.

I saw Vati and Mr. Chang in deep discussion. Fritzi and I spotted an open barrel of unshelled peanuts. Would Mr. Chang or Vati see Fritzi and me if we filled our blue overall jean pockets with peanuts?

Fritzi and I both put a few in our pockets. Realizing this was actually quite simple, we stashed a few more and then some more. Soon all of our pockets were bulging, even the bibs of our blue overalls.

To keep from being spotted, we hunched over between grocery aisles. When we were near to door we ran to the back seat of the car. There we broke peanut shells and munched with contentment.

Did we know we had done wrong? Yes, Yes, Yes. The clues were: 1) how cleverly we hid between the aisles and, 2) how we ate the nuts as we hovered down on the floor of the back seat of the car.

Vati looked all over the grocery store for us and then decided he would see if we were in the car. He opened the door and saw all the peanut shells on floor of the car.

Vati never said a word. He took the four apples from the bag he had just purchased, put them on the seat of the car and handed the bag to the two of us.

"This was not so bad," we thought. "All we have to do is clean up our mess."

"Now," Vati said, "give this bag to Mr. Chang and have him weigh it. Tell him to triple the weight and then, you, Fritzi, figure out how much you two owe him."

I began to cry, but not Fritzi. He is the stoic one, but I could tell he, too felt like a thief. We had to confront Mr. Chang.

"Vati, couldn't you do it for us?" my brother pleaded.

"I am not the one who stole the peanuts. I am not the one who ate the peanuts," he retorted.

As we walked slowly with the bag of evidence, I felt my father's footsteps behind us.

We gave the bag to Mr. Chang. How he looked, I do not know, for Fritzi and I handed over the contraband with heads hug low.

Vati nudged us both with the knuckles of his hand. "Tell Mr. Chang what you did and how sorry you are; then ask for his forgiveness. Tell him you will never, never, never do this again."

Mr. Chang said, "Oh, it's alright."

"No, Mr. Chang, it is not 'alright'; you did NOT get to eat the peanuts either," Vati replied.

Fritzi and muttered about how Mr. Chang was to weight the peanut shells and then charge us three times the value of the peanut shells.

Fritzi began to figure, but each time the answer was not quite right.

"Do it again," Vati said sternly. This time there was no help in solving the problem. He had to do it again and again until he got it right.

On the way home there were no smiles, no laughter, just listening to my father tell us how many dozen eggs we would have to put under the egg candler until the debt was paid off.

Nothing more was ever said, nor needed to be said, about HONESTY, and CHEATING.

I remember it all vividly to this day.

THE BATTLE

A lot of action happens in the corral. Cows nudge one another, the one who wants to be milked first standing by the gate waiting for my father to show up with his bucket and his milking stool. We milked directly out in the corral. We had no milking barn. My father never used hobbles, a device which bound the cow's hind legs and kept her from kicking. Learning how to milk a cow at a young age I, too, soon learned when a cow was about to kick. I saw my father put his forehead on the cow as he milked her. I did the same and soon discovered there was a slight shiver in her nerves just before she attempted to knock over the pail of milk which was just under her udder. I knew that I must immediately put my left arm out to stop the kick. The kicks were often not hard, just intrusive.

My father did use a lasso for the cows who decided that walking about was a good activity while she was being milked. He bound her with the lasso by the neck and tied her to a corral fence post. It seemed to always be the same two or three cows that had walks on their minds. After a few times being tied to the post, they soon learned it was useless and my father no longer used the rope.

One day, Fritzi and I were in the corral watching my father tie a cow we named One Dot to the post. For a reason that I can't recall, Fritzi and I got into a heated argument. Heated arguments between the two of us always end in doubling our fists and coming to blows. Don't feel badly for me; I could hold my own. My father usually let us solve our own problems, but this time I think he had enough. With one swoop he lassoed Fritzi and me and bound us together, hands by our sides, unable to move.

My father tied us to the same post that held One Dot.

"Now you vant to fight, huh. Vell let's see who vill vin, now." My father mocked.

And with that he went on to milk his next cow, one that did not have to be tied to a post. The post and the lasso were well occupied.

"Let me know ven you are friends again and I vill untie you." He remarked sternly.

THE CIRCUS

As a very small child, I once attended a circus. Most farm children would have been in awe of the mysterious looking animals. Their only resemblance to a cow was that they, too, had four legs. My mother clutched my wrist as people pushed and shoved their way to get to the large tent. I could do nothing but cry.

Something must have remained in my subconscious. Sometime later, I decided to have a one-kid circus of my own.

It was my chore to feed the calves. Newborns were taken from their mothers after two days. The first two days the mother's milk still contain a nutrient that served as a natural antibiotic. We were not allowed to ship this enhanced milk. I remember it being a yellowish, brownish, orange color. When the milk had turned its natural whitish color, the babies were removed from their mothers and placed in the "calf pen." Newborns did not naturally know how to drink from a bucket. I watched Vati many times as he instructed me.

"Put the milk in the 'milk bucket' and place your body over its neck," he instructed, "Now slide forward forcing the calf to lower its head, Dip your hand in the milk and quickly insert all your fingers except your thumb into the calf's mouth. Put some more weight on its neck, making your hand go down into the bucket of milk without taking your fingers from its mouth. As it sucks on your fingers, it will take in milk from the bucket. Slyly, remove your fingers. See, it's now drinking on its own. Realize, calves are like children, some learn more quickly than others," he analytically added. "Now it's your turn. Feed this one," he told me.

I followed Vati's instructions step by step. I did run into an obstacle...my legs were not as long as his and 1 didn't have the weight he had. The calf tossed its head and 1 fell, knocking over the remaining milk.

"Keep trying," and with a twinkle in his eye he added, "Children are like calves, some learn more quickly." He walked away, knowing full well that 1 would "get it" sooner or later.

That was the beginning of my circus. If elephants could walk in circles by only the direction of a cracking whip then these calves could also be trained.

At the beginning, l would stand in the middle of the pen, chasing back any calf that wanted my attention. I had the assistance of Amorli, my little, loving dog. He was a fast learner, and quickly surmised the game. We did this for several days until, with a wave of my hand, this herd of highly intelligent calves took their stance at the edge of the pen.

It was now time to advance the instruction. 'If I chased them, would they begin to run in a circle still staying on the outskirts of the pen?' l wondered.

I tried, they did. My next command was to train them to stop at a given signal. I didn't know how to whistle, so I tried a five-syllable yodel. That didn't work so easily, but with the help of Amorli, this task, too, was mastered. We worked on this mission for what seemed like forever until finally the command was learned. Yes, calves are like children--some learn more quickly than others. I began thinking that I should put the learned ones in the lead. What success. What should they learn next?

I remembered that with the crack of whip, the elephants that were going in a circles suddenly did an about face. In unison, they were now going in the opposite direction. Could l train these calves that trick?

Wanting them to be very much like the true circus performers, l got Vati's lasso, whirled it in the air and low and behold, the calves were immediately going in the alternate direction, but they were no longer in single file. Out of fright, the trained calves now wanted to stampede. With practice, though, the calves soon knew that the lasso was a signal and not used for whipping. There was one more step.

Most of the young calves were soon to be heifers, grown as future milk cows. One of the largest and tamest was a bull calf. I soon learned to ride him. Now l was in the middle of the pen, creating a circus of wonder. Benjamin Bullboy appeared to like helping Amorli and me put the little show on the road. Daily l went. Daily I was challenged, but what a circus it was.

I knew it had to end when, at the dinner table, I heard my father say to the hired hand, "I wonder what's happening to this year's herd of calves? They seem to be so skinny. Why aren't they gaining weight?" We are going to have to increase their grain allotment...and the bull calf...why is his back so swayed?" he pondered.

My Mother, the Hay Derrick, and the Mule

Haying was an integral part of a dairy in Imperial Valley, California. Alfalfa was mowed, set in windrows, and left on the ground until it was dry. It was then called hay. The farmer, his team of horses, an empty wooden wagon, and the hired hand, drove to the field to pick up the hay. This precious fodder rolled from the ground to the wagon by way of a mobile conveyer that was attached to the wagon. My father caught the hay and built massive piles to be hauled home when the wagon was full. This was a highly synchronized task. If this chore were done too late in the day the hay would lose precious leaves due to its dryness. Early morning was spent milking the cows and feeding the animals. Somehow my father knew how to work all that in. By evening the dew once again settled on the hay, making its handling easier and with less leaf loss.

When the hay was brought home it then had to be made into a large stack for use when the cows couldn't be sent out to pasture or when there was a shortage of green. Hay was always available for the animals.

Unfortunately, haying time was universal in Imperial Valley. Often there were not enough hands to go around. Consequentially, anyone between the ages of six and eighty was summoned to help.

Unloading the hay was just as tedious as getting it from the field. It involved a minimum of three people. One drove the mule or horse that pulled a cable from a large, large triangular wooden derrick. Attached to this wooden derrick was a huge fork whose tongs probed into the hay and then released the hay from the wagon to a large haystack. The person who manned the mule was my mother. The animal was made to go forward, pulling until the cable was at the correct height to be swung into place by the person manning the drop site. If the mule was not driven far enough the fork load would not be high enough. If the mule went too far....

Once my mother drove the mule too far and the whole derrick came tumbling down, breaking many of the wooden brace bars. Luckily no human or animal was injured.

The following day I saw Mr. Ming, the inventor of the derrick, out by the hay stack surveying the damages. Not wanting the unknown to remain unknown,

I spent the day watching Mr. Ming. At one point he asked me, "What in the world happened here?"

"Oh, my mother and the mule broke it." I responded. The humor of this phrase soon echoed throughout the Swiss community of Imperial Valley.

THE BABY CHICKS

Not only did my father teach us to work, but there was a philosophy behind the work ethic.

"Unless they are ill, people who don't work can't eat." Was one of my father's lectures. He practiced this, he modelled this and he demanded it of Fritzi and me.

Another adage he preached was, "You have choices. If you don't want to spend your life working as a ditch digger, then you had best go to school and develop your brain. There are many ways of earning money. Most of it involves work and the use of your mind."

When I reached the age of twelve my father took me aside and said, "Vreneli, it is time you learned how to make a dime using your brawn and brain." This was the beginning of my chicken business.

Vati (father) took me to the old four-corners of El Centro, California, where a baby chick hatchery thrived. We bought one hundred baby chicks with money I had saved up. Each Christmas, which was also my birthday, my Godfather, Julius Hilfiker, gave me a pair of slippers and in the toe was twenty-five dollars in cash. I saved these twenty-five dollars annually, putting them into savings account at Keith Savage's First National Bank of Holtville, California. It was hard to part with the money, yet I knew anything my father had a hand in would be fruitful.

We brought the newborn chicks home and Vati showed me how to turn on the heat in the brooder that was in the chicken pen, and how to set out the finely chopped meal for them to eat. Water was also put in the pen.

Vati started out by saying, "Use a shallow dish for drinking water and see that it always has water. You do not want to make the dish too deep. The baby chicks could drown or sit in the water and catch a cold. When one chick gets sick others catch the illness and many will die. You do not want that to happen. The more chicks that grow to becoming hens, the more money you will make. Does that make sense?" He questioned.

I beamed at the peeping chicks, knowing that this was not part of digging ditches. I had to work to keep the babies alive and I had to use my mind to remember all Vati had told me.

The test came three nights later, when an unusual rain storm hit Imperial Valley. Although my chicks were in a covered pen, it was not a shelter from cold.

"Put your chicks in the brooder to keep them warm," my father said to me. It was raining, and I somehow figured Vati would go and care for the chicks for me.

A second reminder came with a little harshness of the voice. "Put your chicks in the brooder," he said with emphasis.

I still thought Vati would do the task for me, but he continued to read the Imperial Valley Press.

"I am going to tell you one more time, 'Put the chicks in the brooder,'" he said.

And then came the "teaching/learning" part. "If you lose ten of your one hundred chicks due to the weather, that is one-tenth of your investment. If one-tenth of your investment is gone, you will have lost your profit. That means you spend the whole time of the growth of your chicks, working for nothing," he said. And with that he went back to his newspaper.

I got the message. Shivering, I put on my raincoat, went out to the chicken pen and tended to the chicks.

I had a very profitable chicken-raising season. I did it several years in a row.

Vati's comment, "that means you spend the whole time of the growth of your chicks, working for nothing," still rings in my ears.

A BIG BUSINESS TRANSACTION

My brother, Fritzi, started his own business at the age of fourteen. He had purchased a red Farmall tractor and a mower, which he attached to the tractor.

Fritzi was doing very well, working before and after school and on weekends. All of his money was invested on the farm implements. He soon realized he needed to expand. He needed to buy a rake to gather up the alfalfa he had cut with his mower.

There was a problem... *Money*. Where was he to get the money to buy the rake? He went to our father and asked him what he should do.

"Ah," thought my father, as he rubbed his forehead. "Why don't you ask your sister? She has money saved up from her chicken business."

"Do you think she will give it to me," my brother questioned?

"*Give* it to you?" my father responded. "No, no, no, but she might lend it to you. Go and talk to her."

"What does '*lend*' mean?" my brother wanted to know.

Before long, the three of us were in a questioning dialogue. There was no way I was giving my hard-earned money to Fritzi. Then came the word 'lend' to my ears. It sounded an awful lot as if I were still giving my money away.

My father sat us down at the kitchen table. In front of us we each had a pencil and a piece of paper.

First, my father wanted to make sure he had our attention. Then his comments began. "'*Lending*' is NOT giving your money away. When you '*lend*' money you want to make a '*profit*.'" When you make a '*profit*' you get back more *money than you gave the person. The added money is your 'profit.*'"

"Oh, wow!" I thought that is a lot easier than raising chickens. "Can I get twice as much back as I give Fritzi?," I asked my father.

"Not usually," my father replied. "That would be greedy."

"How do we determine for how much to ask?" I wanted to know. Now my head was spinning. I could 'lend' money *and* raise chickens. I could see dollar signs.

"Bankers talk about '*percent*' and '*rate*' when they lend money. A '*percent*' is usually a part of one dollar. That part is then called the '*rate*'. '*Rates*' are listed in the financial, the business section of our local Imperial Valley newspaper. Let's get *The Imperial Valley Press* newspaper and see what today's rate is," my father continued.

All this time Fritzi was silent. He was a thinker. He was listening. He was digesting all that was said. He was way ahead of me. Of course, he was older. He was to be the *borrower* and I the *lender*. These terms were soon part of our vocabulary.

Fritzi and I agreed on a rate, but this was just the beginning of our financial realm. "Tomorrow we will go to Holtville, a little town not too far from where we lived. We will go to see Keith Savage, the president of our small bank," he told the two of us.

"I thought Fritzi was borrowing money from me, NOT from The First National Bank of Holtville."

"It will all start to fall into place when we talk to Mr. Savage," my father stated.

It was a balmy summer morning and after the cows were milked, the animals were fed, and the morning chores were done, we cleaned up, got into our Chevy, and headed for Holtville. We parked directly across from the Holtville bank, by the city park, crossed the street, and entered the bank.

Mr. Savage spotted us immediately and shook hands with my father. "What can I do for you today, Mr. Kuhn?" he asked.

"I need one of your loan application forms, if you could spare one?" my father responded.

"Are you wanting to borrow some money from our bank, Mr. Kuhn? Let's have a seat in my office and we will discuss rates." Mr. Savage was a friendly bank president who knew all the farmers and was always eager help them with their business.

"No, Mr. Savage, I would just like a blank application form. I need to look one over," my father continued.

Keith Savage looked puzzled, but complied. My father shook his hand, thanked him, and we were on our way home.

Again we were seated at the breakfast table wondering how the next part of this the story would unfold. "Before we begin I need to explain something to you two. There is more than one kind of a loan."

And so began the conversation about *simple interest, compound interest,* and *balloon payments.* Fritzi immediately realized that compound interest was out of the question. I preferred the balloon payment because I would not continually have to collect and deposit money in the bank and, furthermore, I did not need the money until I had to buy baby chicks again.

Fritzi and I agreed on a balloon payment which would become due exactly in nine month when I need the money. We both decided on a three percent interest rate. Vati made Fritzi fill out the paper, and with his guidance all the while explained it all to me. Except for giving Fritzi the money, I thought the deal was done.

"Oh, no!" said my father. "Now I want each of you to look deeply in one another's eyes and culminate this part of the deal with a handshake."

Again both Fritzi and I wanted to know the importance of a handshake.

"When one has good and honest intentions in starting a business deal one always shakes hands. This signifies an air of trust. Are you two good and honest people and are you dealing in an air of trust? If so, shake hands," my father sternly stated.

We did.

I asked my father if he would call Mr. Savage for me, and ask him if he would transfer the money from my savings account into Fritzi's account, to which Vati replied, "It's your business, it's your deal, it's your job, *you* do it."

And so Vati called Mr. Savage to make the money transfer.

Exactly Nine Months Later

Fritzi was now more deeply in the hay harvesting business, having fully paid for his Farmall tractor, mower, AND hay rake.

My calendar had been marked. Days before I reminded my brother of the upcoming repayment date. Fritzi asked my father if he would talk to Mr. Savage to transfer the money and profit into my account, to which Vati replied, "It's your business, it's your deal, it's your job, *you* do it."

All the business transactions were culminated. My father praised us for a business transaction well done. Fritzi and I thought this was closure, but, Oh, no—there was one more phase.

"Vreneli, get the loan application and call your brother," my father commanded.

"Why, what are we doing, now?" I asked quizzically.

"You will see," Vati responded

In one hand I held the contract and in the other I held on to my father's hand. Fritzi followed. Vati took us out to the chicken pen. On the back side of the pen my father asked Fritzi to dig a hole. Not knowing what the hole was for, but with respect, Fritzi took his bare hands and made a pit.

"Is this big enough?" Fritzi asked.

"That is a perfect hole," Vati responded, and with that he took from his Levi pants, a match from a packet he often used to light his smoking pipe. "Vreneli, you hold the loan document over the hole and Fritzi, you ignite the match and begin to burn the paper. When the flames start. drop the loan paper into the hole," my father instructed.

We did as we were told. When the paper was completely burned, Vati asked me to cover the ashes and fill the hole with dirt.

"Perhaps you are both wondering about the importance of the task we just performed. You see," my father continued, "when a transaction is complete we must destroy the contract, for it has no more value. We don't want someone to come back years later with a document that has completely been satisfied by both parties, namely Fritzi and Vreneli," my father told us.

"There is one more important clause to the culmination of this business contract, and that is for you two to shake hands once more. Do you know why you must repeat this gesture?" he asked.

Both of us knew...

to validate that this was a good, honest,
and trusting business transaction.

A Pondering Purchase

Living on a farm gives one many opportunities to ponder, question, learn, and come up with new ideas. This was a frequent quest of mine. It wasn't that I had immediate solutions. More often the questioning puzzle expanded. Such was the case when my father asked me to accompany him to a farm auction.

Mr. Riechter, an Imperial Valley farmer, was selling his farm animals and farm equipment. Among the many things for sale were his milk cows. I watched my father as he bid on several cows. Other bids topped his bid. Up for auction came a Holstein with markings unlike our herd. Our cows were white with two to three large black blotches. This cow was painted like a beautiful Dalmatian. Perhaps because she did not look like the rest of Mr. Riechter's herd, no one bid on her. My father made a bid.

We took the cow home and named her Riechter. And here the puzzle began. Normally when a new animal is brought into the herd a "pecking" order takes place. Within two to three days the new animal is accepted into the family. Not so with Riechter. She was butted, kicked and pushed. Each day was like the one before

Riechter, not wanting to engage, found a lonely corner of the corral. The elite milk cows luxuriously grouped around the water tank and the eucalyptus trees. Riechter came to the water tank, took a few gulps, and went back to the hot, sunny corner of her domain.

About a year later Riechter gave birth to a calf, one marked just as she was marked. She nursed her in the sunny heat. Three days later, my father took Riechter's calf and put her in the pen with the other little calves, as is customary on the dairy farm. Daily I went to see if the little calf was accepted by the others. Daily I saw her jump and play with the little calves. There were no signs of rejection.

Several years later the calf, now a heifer was soon to give birth to her own new little one. She was brought into the pen and was given the same treatment as her mother. In the corner of the corral, I observed three generations... three generations of rejection.

What do I make of these observations? As a young child I pondered and pondered and I am still questioning. Do animals have a sense of prejudgment? Was this all a coincidence? How does this relate to mankind? What have I learned from this?

The Golden Necklace

If only this golden necklace could talk. What a story it would have to tell. Knowing this is not possible this writer must tell the story as best she can.

The golden necklace was laced with three individual loops with three loops intertwined. With age a few of the loops were missing, but because there were three to each loop the chain still held together. The chain easily wrapped around my neck three times. It was a beautiful but simple necklace made of gold.

The necklace is an heirloom handed down to my mother by her mother, who in turn got it from her mother. Obviously, it goes back several generations. How old it really is we do not know. Each of the intertwined chains was handmade and hand assembled.

In my mother's family there were four sisters. Why my mother, Ida Glattli, was given the chain and not any of the other sisters, I do not know.

When my mother came to the United States, she brought this treasure with her. It was stored in the bank vault and was taken out only for a rare occasions, or to be cleaned…except for one interesting moment.

My mother had asked my father for some money to spend…I know not for what.

"This is a time of Depression", Vati reminded my mother, " and money was not to be spent senselessly."

What did my mother do? She took the necklace to the local pawn shop and exchanged it for money. Now she could buy what she felt she so desperately needed.

My father was furious. He headed straight down to the pawn shop and paid for this heirloom treasure. The pawn broker had no idea what a personal treasure he handed over to my father. And I have no idea how much my father paid for it. I never asked, but now he knew it was his.

Years later, when my own children were in their teens, Vati gave me the golden necklace telling me that I should think of cutting it, giving each of the girls half of the chain.

"Vati, that would not do justice to such an heirloom. I will keep it and then decide which of my girls shall have it to pass on to one of her children or grandchildren," I told my father.

As my children married, I decided to give it to Diane. She is the one with much sentiment. It became a Christmas gift and I detected enormous gratitude, delight and pleasure. Jacki, too, was in agreement that it was to go to Diane, who should keep it. Diane has two boys. I don't think she will pass it on to them. Jacki has no children.

I feel very strongly who will get the golden necklace, but I won't share that. From the Heaven's above I shall smile and say, "Good, choice, Diane and whoever gets the treasure . . . the story must goes on."

A Mischievous Twinkle in His Eyes

My father loved life. He loved to dance, he loved to sing and yodel, and he loved a glass of wine with a good, home-cooked meal that he most likely hunted or fished for himself and then cooked in his kitchen. He was a master at them all.

At times my father amused himself by concocting his own shenanigans, some of which were quite entailed. A book or movie could have been made of his mischiefs.

Such was the case one September during deer hunting season. He went out to hunt and was unsuccessful. Among the trees, however, he encountered a group of wild burros.

My father's mind began to see a trail that led to a marvelous prank. He shot one, leaving its head behind. Knowing that all bucks shot had to be "deer tagged" and taken into the California ranger station to be registered. My father's brain went into high gear, he placed the tag on the hind leg and soon entered the ranger station.

Vati opened the trunk of the Chevrolet, hoping the ranger would only look at the tag. That is just what the young man did, but then he said, "I thought deer had split hooves?"

"That is true," my father confirmed, "But this is a mule deer."

"Oh," the young man responded, "I've never heard of a mule deer."

But that was only the beginning of my father's merrymaking. He took the meat home, butchering it as only my father knew how. He cut the flesh into pieces and put them all in a large white crockpot. Next he put in spices, garlic, onions and a couple gallons of red wine. In Swiss this was called *hirsch Pfeiffer*. This all needed to sit for several days. When it was thoroughly marinated, Vati got in touch with his good friend, Clem Mueller, Sr. Albert Mueller, and many others of his Swiss buddies to a feast of hirsch fpeiffer. Clem and his wife, Mary, volunteered the festivities at their house. They had a big yard and an outside patio.

As I remember, many people celebrated my father's "hunting success" and his fabulous ability to cook the tasty "deer" meat.

Some time later the Swiss in Holtville, California got wind of the prank. Some found humor in it all and others not so much.

My father, after that, confessed that he always suspected Clem and Mary would invite him over to their home for a "cat" dinner.

My Father and the Construction

of the All-American Canal

During the Depression, the building of the All-American canal was quite a feat for the Imperial Valley. The Imperial Valley is in the most southern part of California, joining the Mexican border. Prior to the All-American Canal, the Imperial Valley had a meager amount of water funneled from the Alamo Canal. The Alamo Canal was but fourteen miles in length and the major part of it was imbedded in Mexicali, Mexico.

The All-American Canal used a gravity flow to derive its water from the Colorado River. The Canal is eighty miles long and has a width of up to two hundred feet and in places is twenty-one feet in depth. It was built between 1934 and 1939. The first flow of water came to the arid desert in 1940. It irrigates over 660,000 acres of land.

The All-American Canal was financed by the United States Bureau of Reclamation (USBR) and was subject to a fifty year contract to be paid for by the Imperial Irrigation District (IID). The final payment was made by the IID in 1994.

What the water from the All-American Canal gave to this Valley, California, The United States of America, and the world, was an abundance of food. It turned a desert wasteland into a "food factory." Farmers built their own ditches that carried the water to their fields. One could begin to see fields of carrots, lettuce, milo, broccoli, citrus trees, nut trees, sugar beets, cotton, and much more. Alfalfa was a major crop serving as fodder for horses, mules, cows, goats, sheep, and pigs. Most farmers also had their own poultry.

And so began my father's involvement in the All-American Canal.

The government had contacted my father to ask if they could lease his draft horses and mules. We had four work horses and two mules. The government wanted to know if we had any farm implements that would be of use in digging the canal. We had two fresnoes; one large and a small one. A fresno is a large, scoop that we used for picking up and hauling off manure. The manure we put on our fields as a powerful fertilizer for our crops. The fresnoes would be of help in moving dirt to construct the All-American Canal.

What my father said to the government was this: there is a major stipulation. If the teams and the fresnoes were to be leased they had to also hire Sunny Brook, the Native American Indian who worked for us. Sunny Brook was his nickname and he loved his whiskey. His real name was Ernest Finley. My father knew that Sunny Brook was the only man that could be trusted with the animals. He catered to the teams as if they were his own, oiling the harnesses daily to soften them so they would not rub wounds into the flesh of the horses and mules.

I don't know what kind of a monetary arrangement my father made with the government, but I do know that once my father took me out to see the building of the canal, Sunny Brook, the teams of animals and the fresnoes were making a big cloud of dust. The All American Canal was being build by native Imperial Valley people along with others.

Quips of Wisdom

There is a story to fit each of my father's quips. I still listen to them and learn. Following are a few of them, along with the story.

Quip 1

When my daughter, Jackalynn, was in her teens, she took great pride in her appearance. This included her fingernail upkeep.

One day as she was buffing and shaping her nails, she decided to polish them a beautiful red. My father looked at her in awe and then said, "Well, young lady, with nails like that, you had better study hard in school, because it is plain to see you won't be using your hands to make a living."

Quip 2

My father was opposed to young teens wearing "war paint," such as lipstick. At times I would put it on after leaving the house.

One day when arriving home, I forgot to remove my "war paint," only to find my father greeting me at the door. He took one look at me and said, "It is impossible to tell the difference between you and your brother's red Farmall tractor."

Quip 3

Another time, when I displayed a strong air of pomposity, my father remarked, "As long as you keep your nose up in the air, you will never see the dime someone dropped on the road."

Quip 4

The little town of Holtville, California, had a large swimming pool, which we referred to as The Holtville Plunge. In the summer, on special occasions we would meet our friends, the Steiners. It was there that I learned to swim almost before I could walk.

The plunge had a regular diving board that we all used over and over, but next to it was a tall, tall, tall diving board for experts. "Jump off of the big diving board and I will give you a quarter," my father said.

I climbed the stairs to the top, I know not how many times, always scaling the rungs back down. My father's quarter was safe in his pocket. "I can do this!" I said to myself and up the ladder I went once more. I looked to make sure my father saw me. Of course, I know now that he saw me each time I went up to the diving board.

I bounced and jumped up and down as I saw the adults do just before they sailed into the water. I stopped and did it again. Again, I checked to see that Vati, my father, was watching me. "It is now or never," I heard myself say...and off I went, into the water, paddling my way up into the air. "That was not hard at all," I thought.

I ran to retrieve my quarter and as Vati handed me the money, I said, "Watch me; for another quarter I will do it again."

"Not so fast, Vreneli. The first quarter you earned, the second would have no learning value. One must work for money. That second jump is NOT work." And that was the end of the discussion.

Quip 5

Living on a farm gave Fritzi and me many opportunities to learn about life. We were always there to do our share, whether it was driving a team of horses up a steep ditch bank or reining them home with a full wagon of hay.

My father once said, "When the load is too tough to pull, always encourage the horse that pulls the most." And then he added, "He who works the hardest, gets the job done." What a life lesson.

Quip 6

My father suffered from a heart condition but never moaned and groaned about it. As he grew older, he did periodically see a physician.

"Mr. Kuhn", the doctor said, "You must no longer drink any alcohol. It is bad for your heart."

"No more coffee royals?" my father sadly asked. A coffee royal is a coffee with brandy, a drink the Swiss all love, and that includes my father. Vati's choice of alcohol in his coffee was a brand labeled Christian Brothers. Vati referred to it as "his brothers."

After some haggling, my father and the doctor agreed Vati could have one teaspoon of Christian Brothers in his coffee, BUT only one.

So what did my father do? He took ONE tea-spoon, turned it upside down and poured the Christian Brothers into his coffee.

Quip 7

In my childhood, there was always something to do. We never knew what a "robe" was. When it was time to get up, we changed from pajamas into work clothes. We never wore a robe.

One day I felt I really had nothing to do that day. Vati walked into my room wanting to know why I was not yet dressed.

"But, Vati, today I have nothing to do, so I am staying in bed," I said.

"Nothing to do? Nothing to do? there is always something to do," Vati chided.

"What do I have to do?" I pleaded.

"You have to get up and make your bed," he remarked.

Quip 8

On our farm we had a house that had a cellar. In it were several wine barrels containing homemade wine. When my father's Swiss friends came, they always ended up in the cellar. In the cellar were some pretty, clean, long-stemmed wine glasses that my father offered to his friends. My father opened the nozzle of the wine drum and filled each person's glass. Then, from the back of the barrel, my father got another glass, one with a beautiful vessel, but the foot of the stem was gone.

"Why do you drink from that glass and not one of these nice ones?" his friend Clem Mueller asked.

"Oh, if my wine glass has no foot, I can't set it down, and so I always have my wine with me," he gleefully retorted.

CONCLUSION

What I have learned from my father is unmeasurable. Much of it is very subtle. Perhaps it was ingrained upon reception and digested throughout my life. I must say, having written this book has brought it all into a reality that enables me to reach a realm of gratitude that is unmeasurable.

I remember my father as a remarkable cook. As he cooked, he held a glass of wine in his hand, had a kitchen towel hanging from his shoulder, and continually tasted what was on the stove or in the oven to confirm that the spices, herbs, salts, pepper, and wine were doing their job. If you watched my father, you could see the twinkle in his eyes, as each meal was a birth of its own.

I remember my father making pigs' ears. Diane and Jacki, my two daughters, looked in awe.

"What is that, Grandpa?" Diane asked.

"Would you like to try it?" my father responded.

The girls went outside, each munching on a pig's ear. At that same time Mr. LeFevre was fixing a broken water pump for my father.

"What are you two eating?" Mr. LeFevre wanted to know.

"Oh, it's so good," Diane said. "Grandpa said it was 'Swiss Steak.'"

My father was also a lover of life. He loved to dance, yodel, and sing. He loved people and was comfortable with the teens, the young, and the oldsters. He was a listener but always had a story to tell. When one of these stories began, he paused, smacked his lips, and slowly began the story. He knew how to pause, how to hold your attention, and then go on with the happenings of the story. My friend Helen Steiner said that I must write in my book about Vati's story telling. Hopefully that is one of the facts this book expresses.

This book was written for my children, my grandchildren, and my great-grandchildren. May they gain kernels of value through their reading, as I did directly from Vati.

ABOUT THE AUTHOR

Dr. Vreneli Kuhn Wilson was born and grew up in Imperial Valley, a farming community in the most southern part of California. Although both of her parents were multilingual, Dr. Wilson did not speak English until she started school.

Dr. Wilson attended San Diego State University and the University of San Diego. She earned a Doctorate Degree from Northern University in Flagstaff, Arizona.

Dr. Wilson taught at McCabe Union School, a country school, and Seeley Union School, both schools being in Imperial Valley. In the 1970's she moved to San Diego, California, where she served as a project director for the San Ysidro School District and as a specialist in reading in Encinitas, California.

After obtaining her Doctorate in Education, Dr. Wilson opened a clinic in Cardiff, California for children with learning disabilities, as well as for gifted and for non-English speaking children.

At present, Dr. Wilson still works individually with children and spends much of her time writing. She has three other books available on Amazon: *Hand-Me-Down Hannah*, a children's beginning reader, and *Hipolito*, a children's book written in Spanish. She also co-authored *Baja California, Land of Contrast.*

27780166R00043

Made in the USA
Columbia, SC
02 October 2018